This book b_____

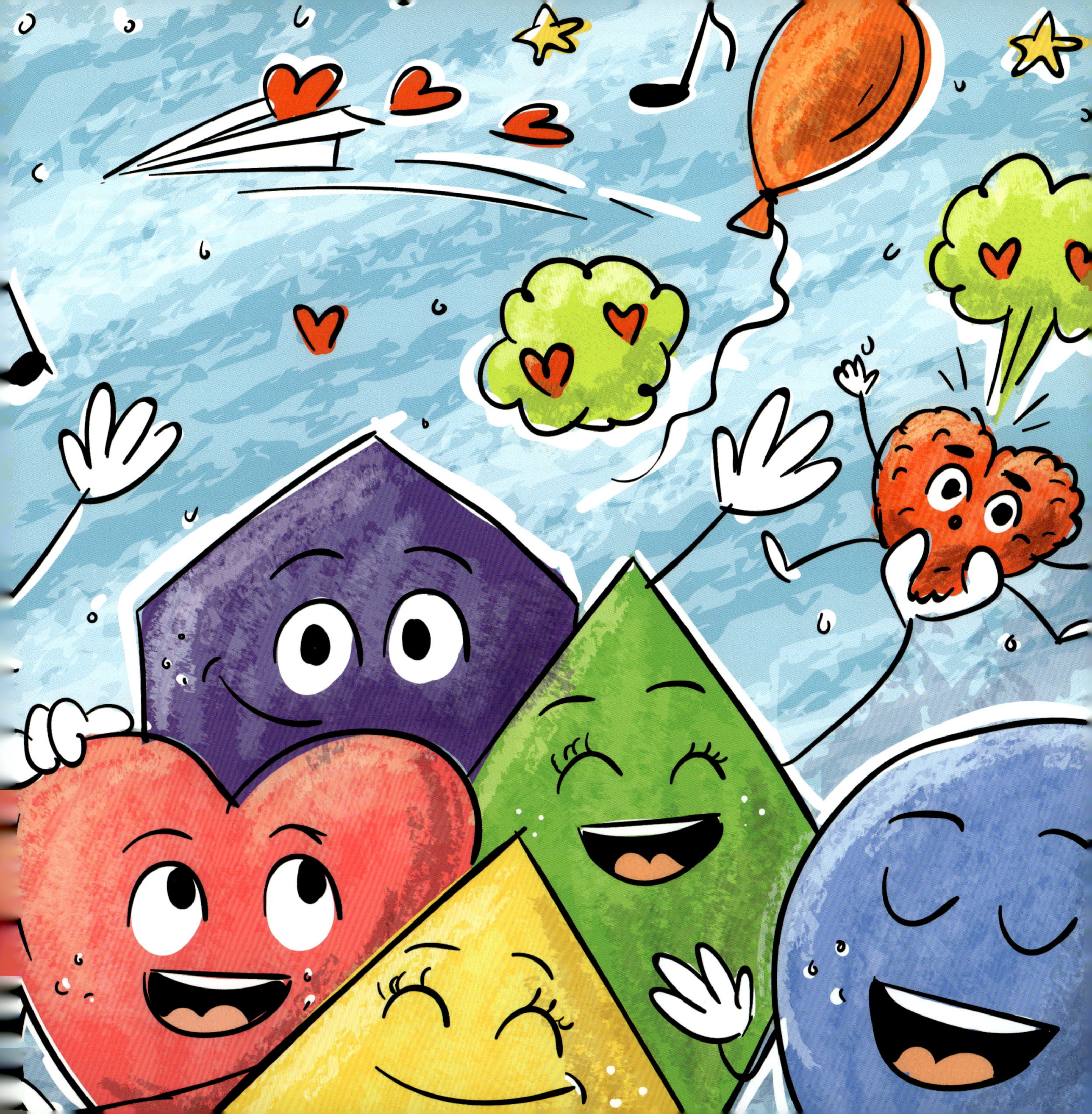

Copyright © 2021 Humor Heals Us. All rights reserved. No part of this book may be reproduced in any form without permission in writing from the publisher. Please send bulk order requests to Humorhealsus@gmail.com Printed and bound in the USA. humorhealsus.com 978-1-63731-320-6

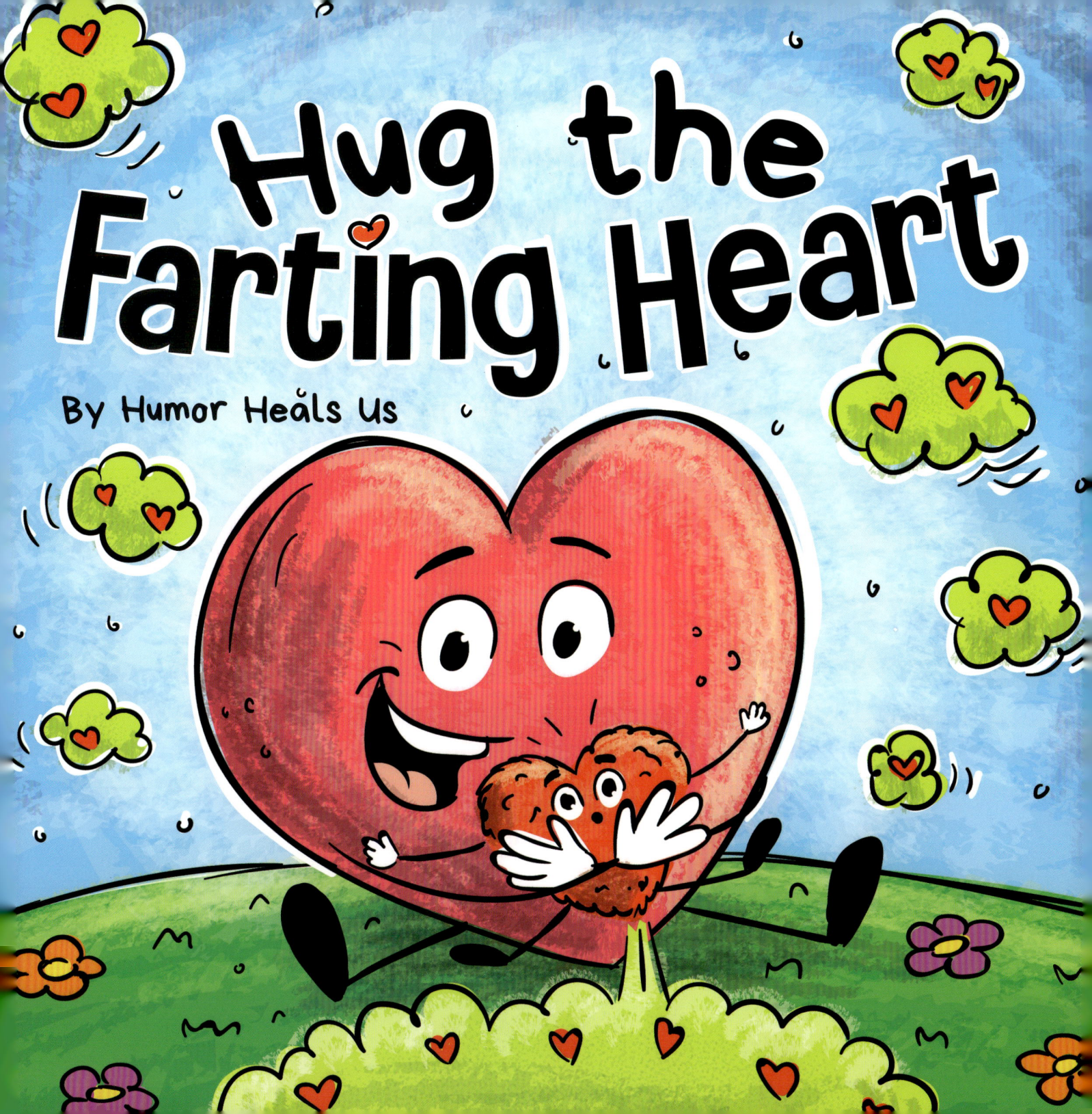

Hug the Farting Heart

By Humor Heals Us

Valentine's Day is a day for **Love**,
For tenderness and care.
It's a day for celebrating those important to you,
Filled with joy and kisses to share.

It's a day for song and chocolate,
For teddy bears and balloons.
It's a day for finding **special** ways
For love to fill a room.

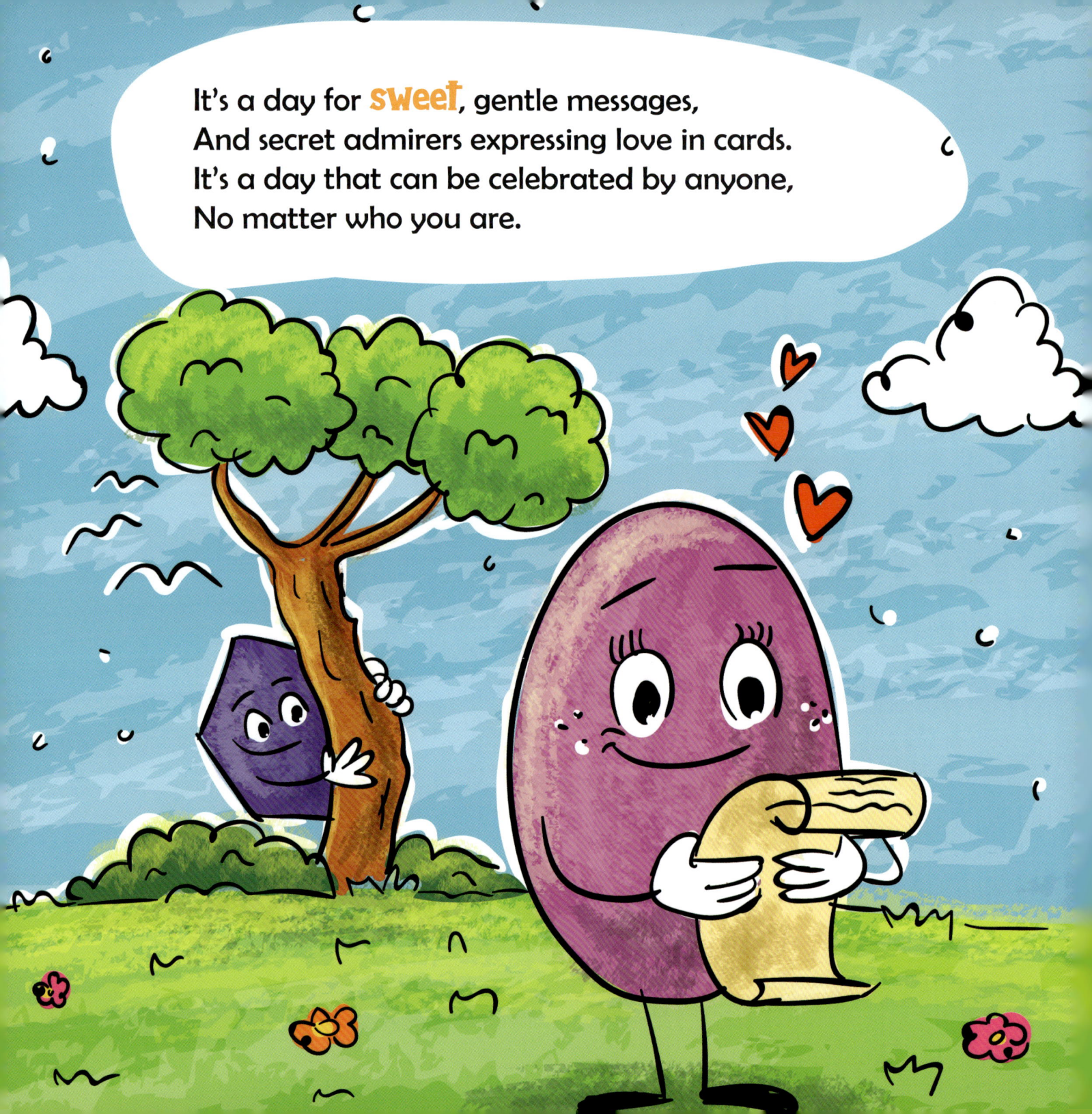

It's a day for **sweet**, gentle messages,
And secret admirers expressing love in cards.
It's a day that can be celebrated by anyone,
No matter who you are.

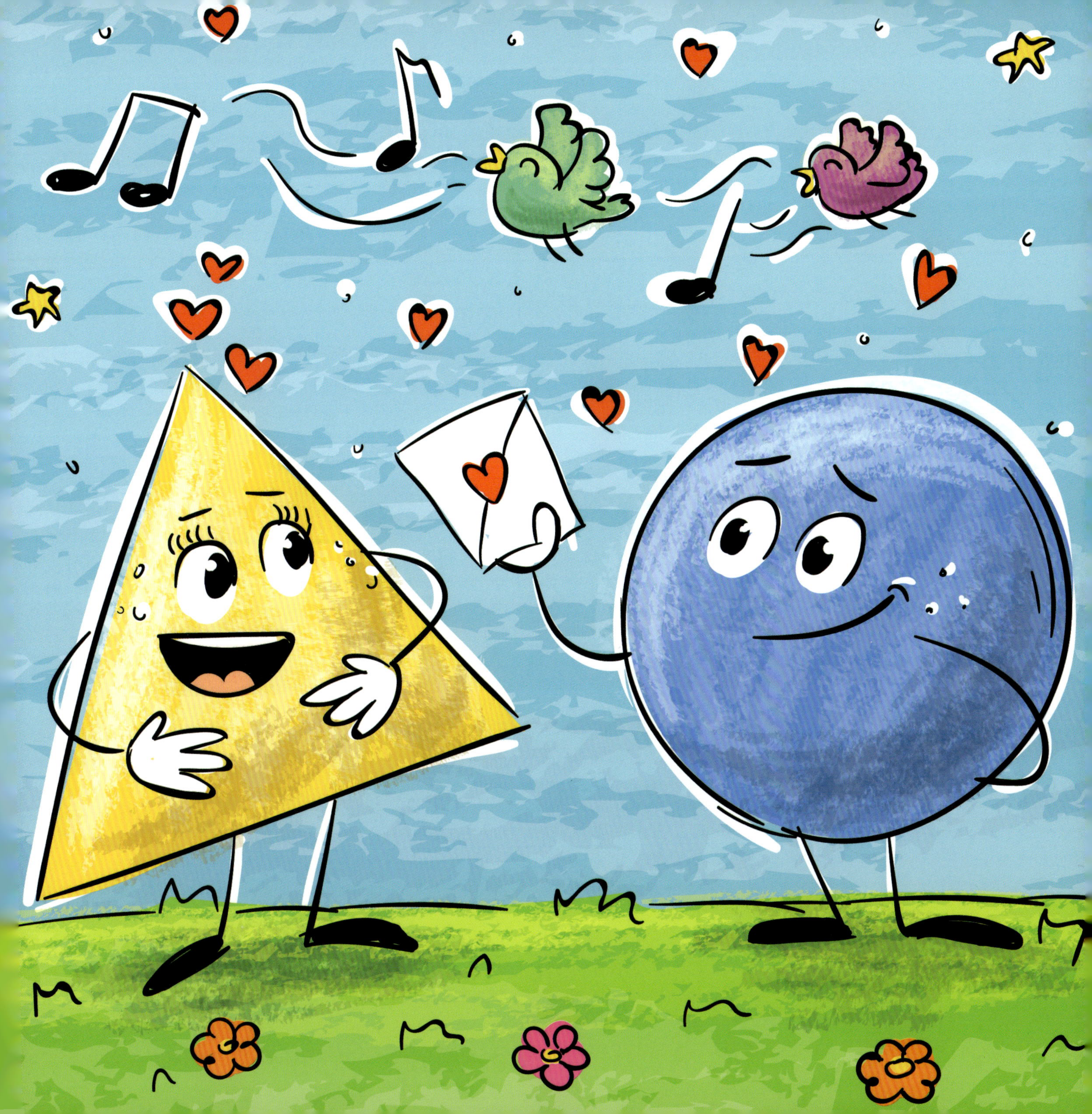

But it can also be a day for silliness,
From the moment that it starts,
Especially when you celebrate it
By **hugging** Hug the Farting Heart.

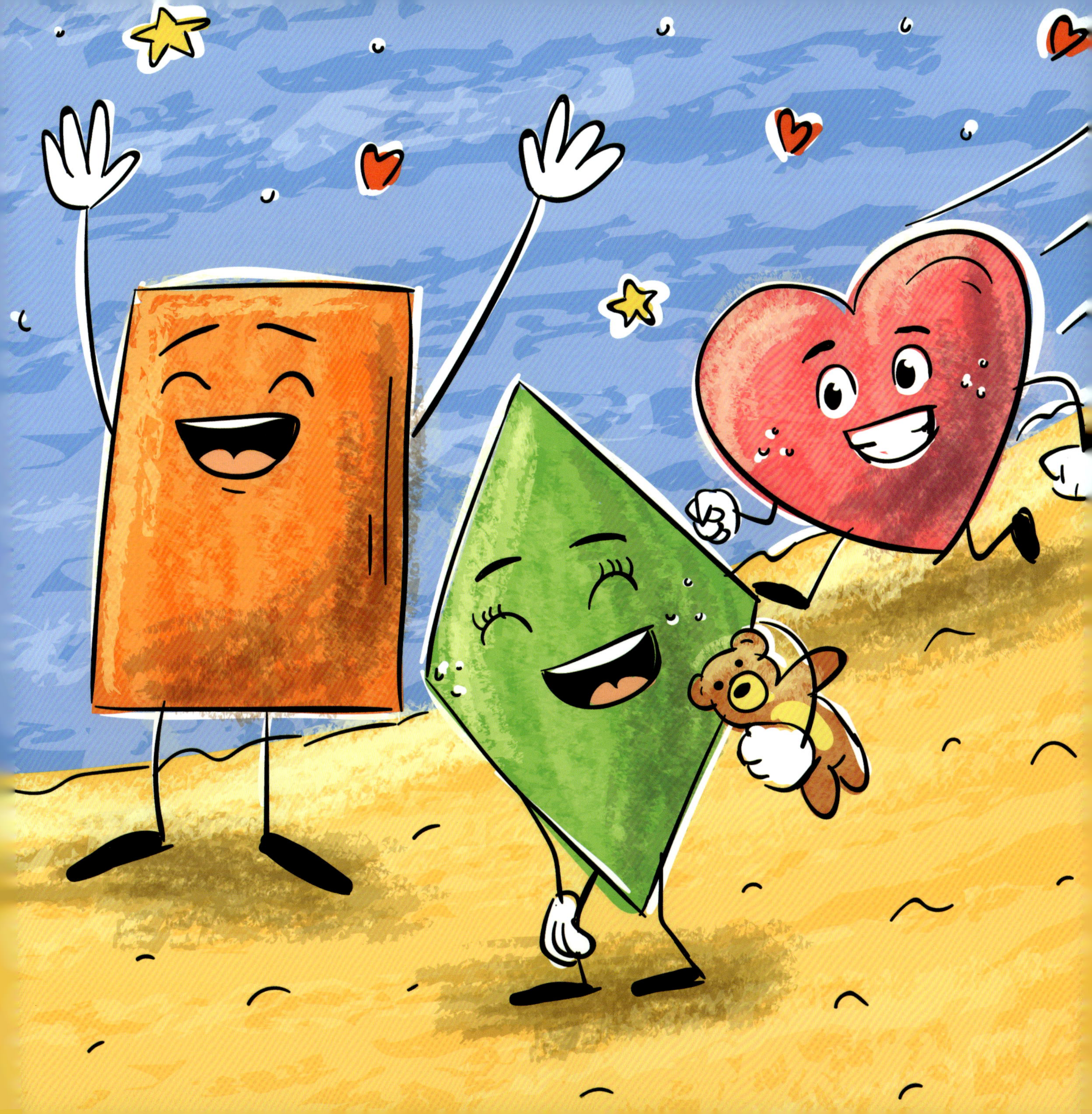

What's a farting heart, you say?
Well it's exactly as it seems.
A farting heart is a big huggable stuffy
You tell all your hopes and **dreams**.

You confide in it all your wishes,
All your desires and what you need.
You tell your heart what's important to you,
And it loves to hear you **read**.

It's there to hear your songs,
The thoughts swirling in your **head**.
It's perched up on your bookshelf during the day,
But at night it joins you in bed.

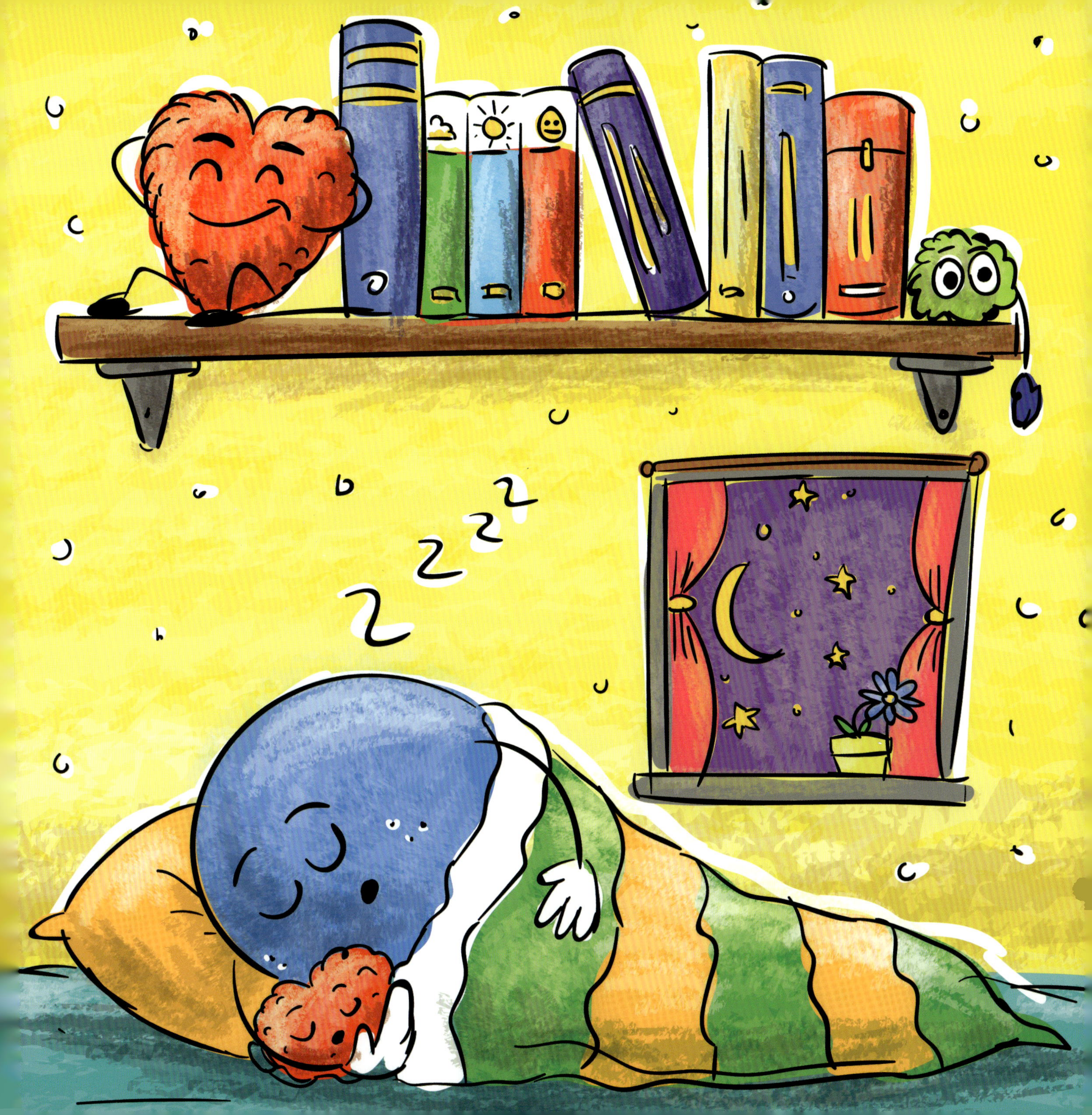

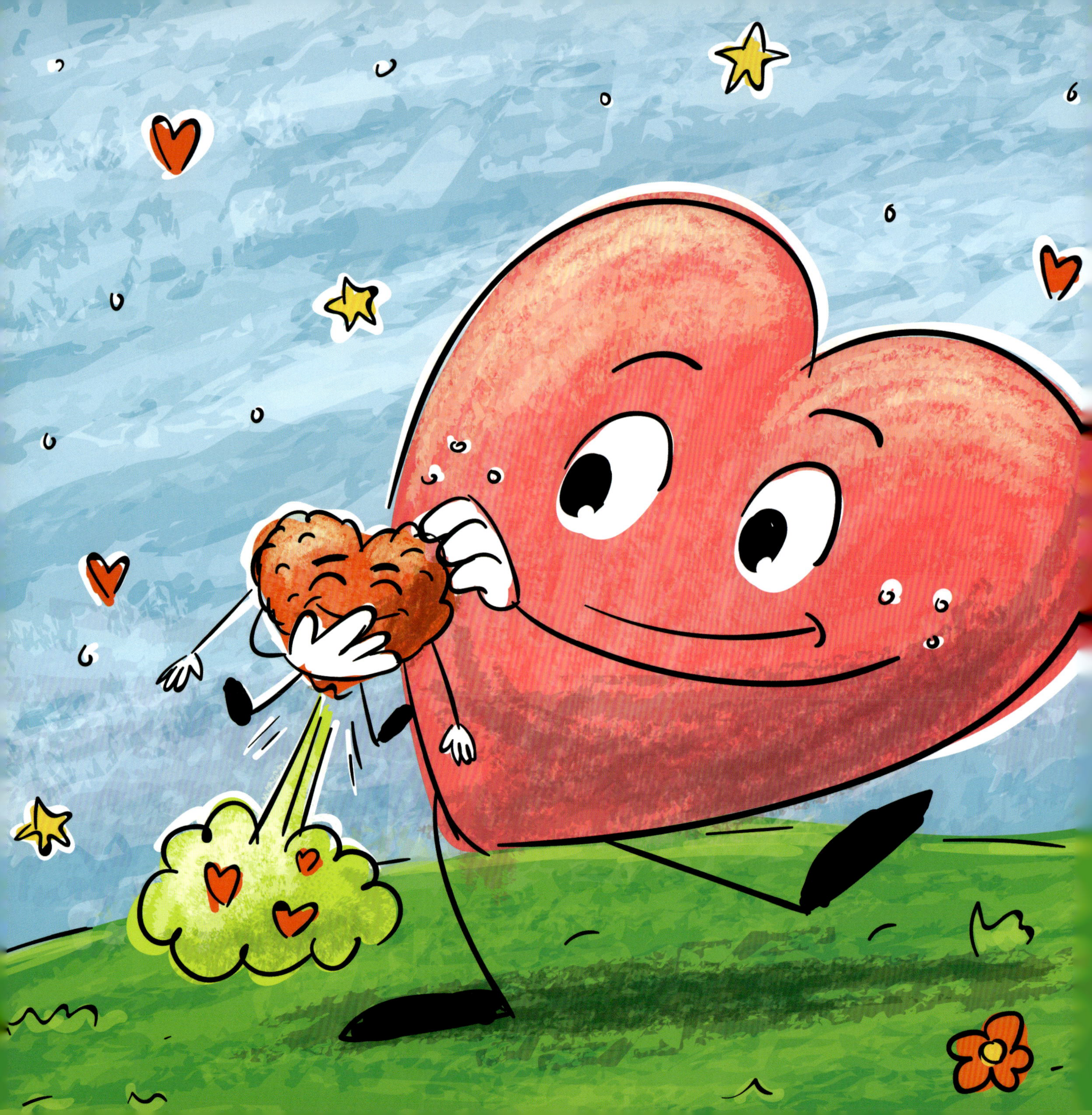

It's **squishy** and extra soft,
Running your hand over it feels so nice.
The heart doesn't mind if you pat its head
Once or even twice.

It loves to be brought on **trips**
Or be buckled in its seat in the car.
The heart is happy to travel,
No matter how near or far.

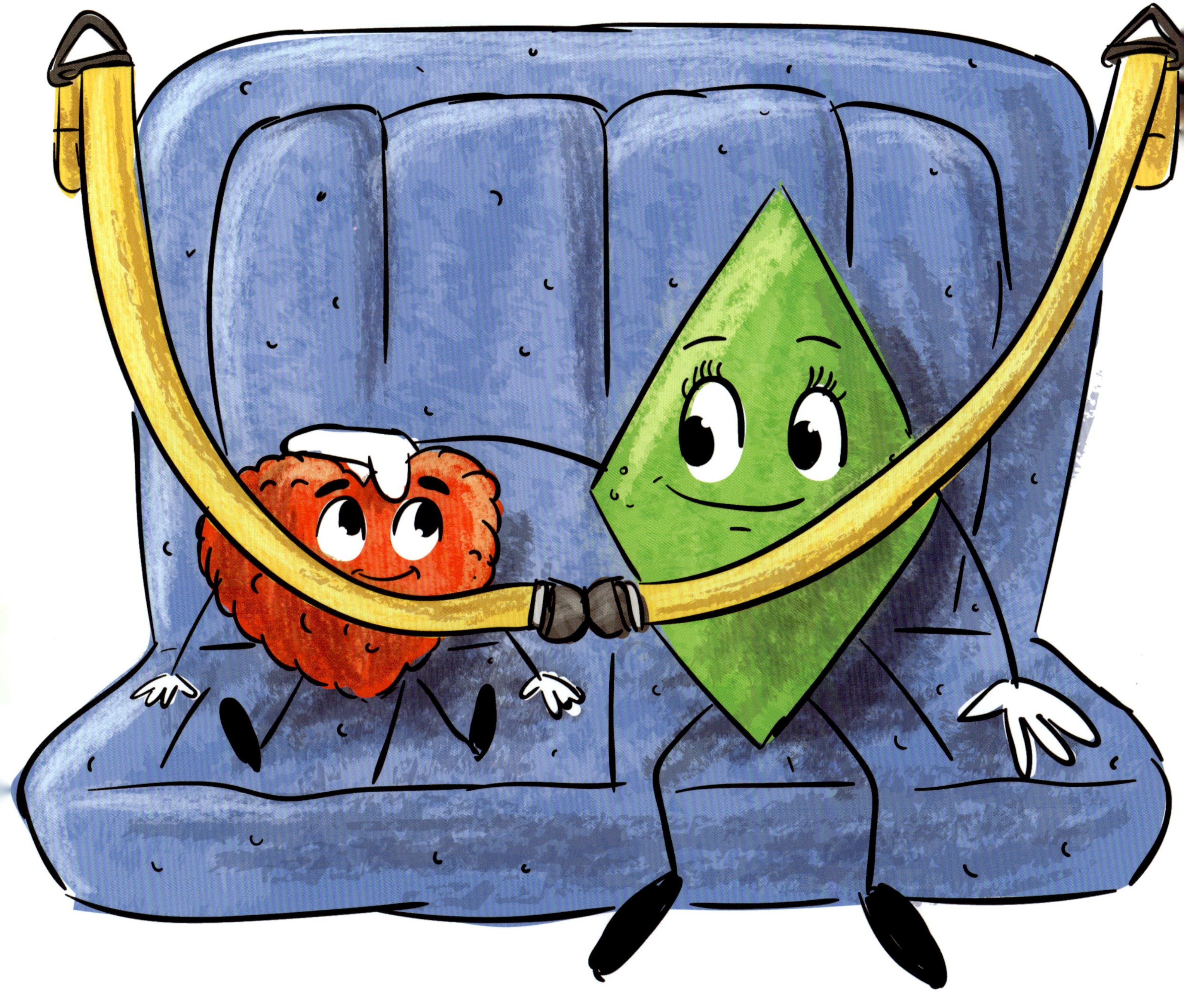

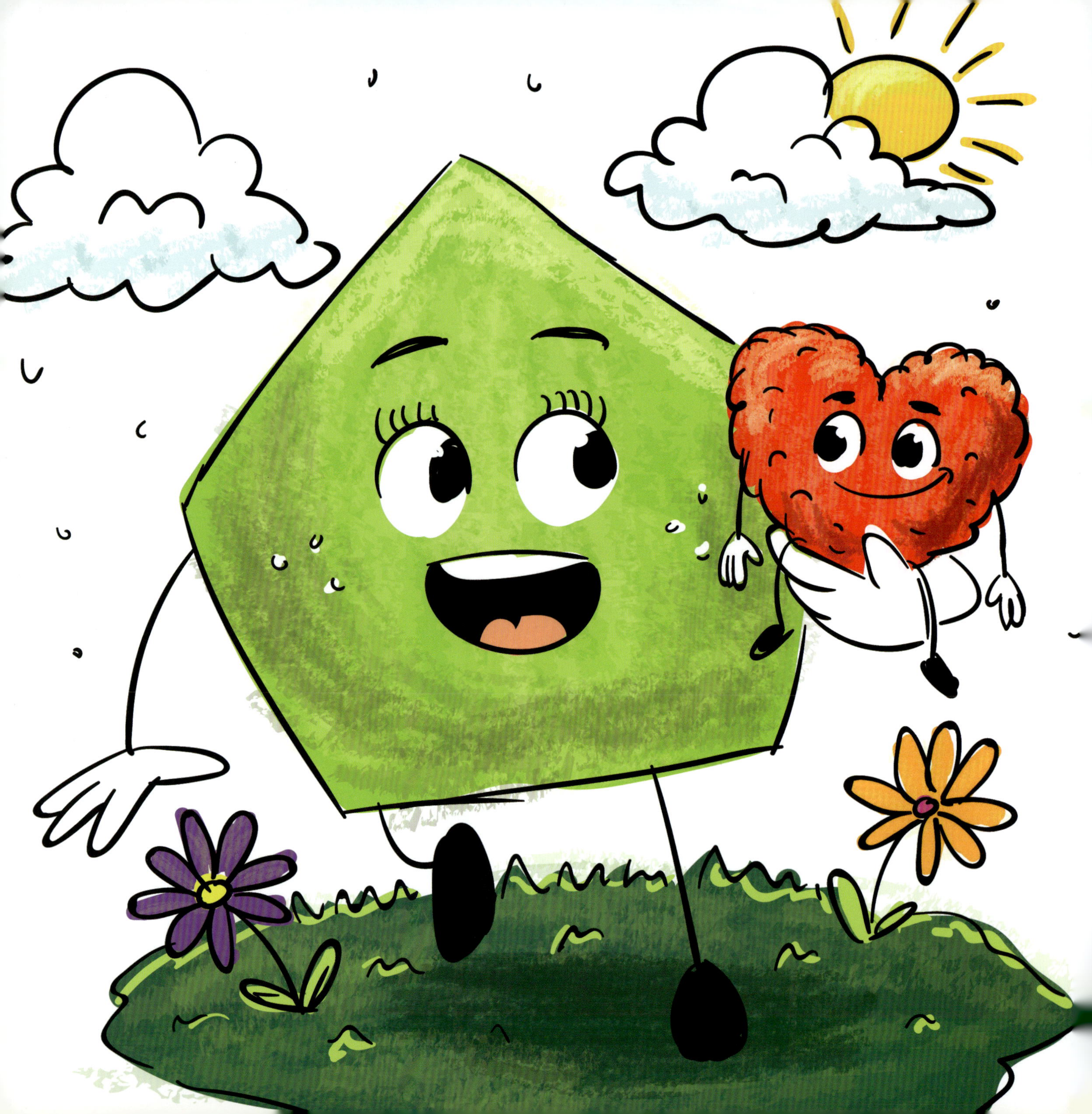

You spend lots of time with your heart,
But you don't hug it everyday.
For if you do, you'll soon remember,
Your heart expresses itself back in a **funny** way.

It shares its love in toots,
Your heart's love language is **farts**.
Its stinky, loud noises
Are something of an art.

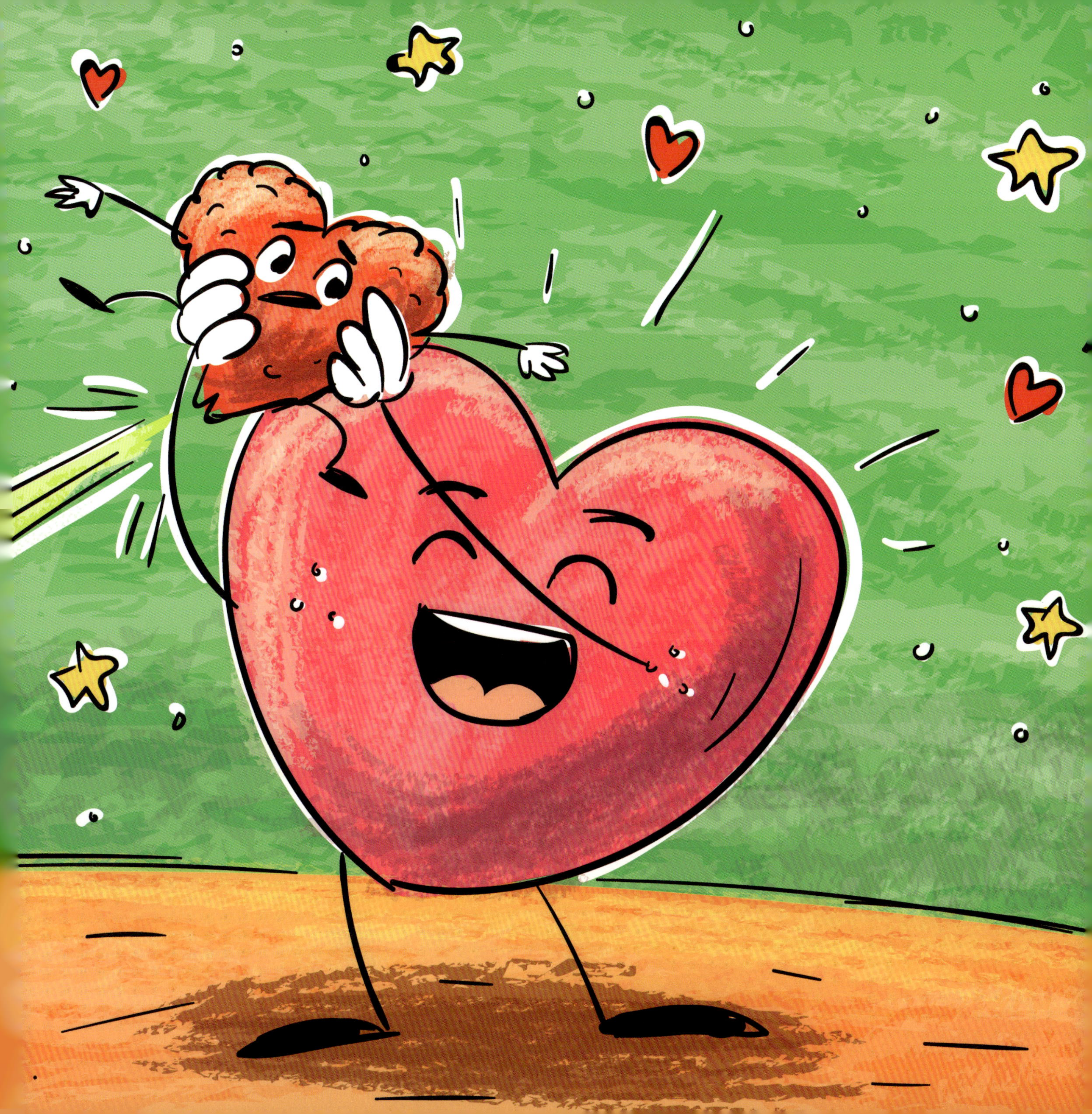

It's not every day a stuffy
Performs a bodily task.
But your silly, smelly heart,
Well, it's got a lot of **gas**!

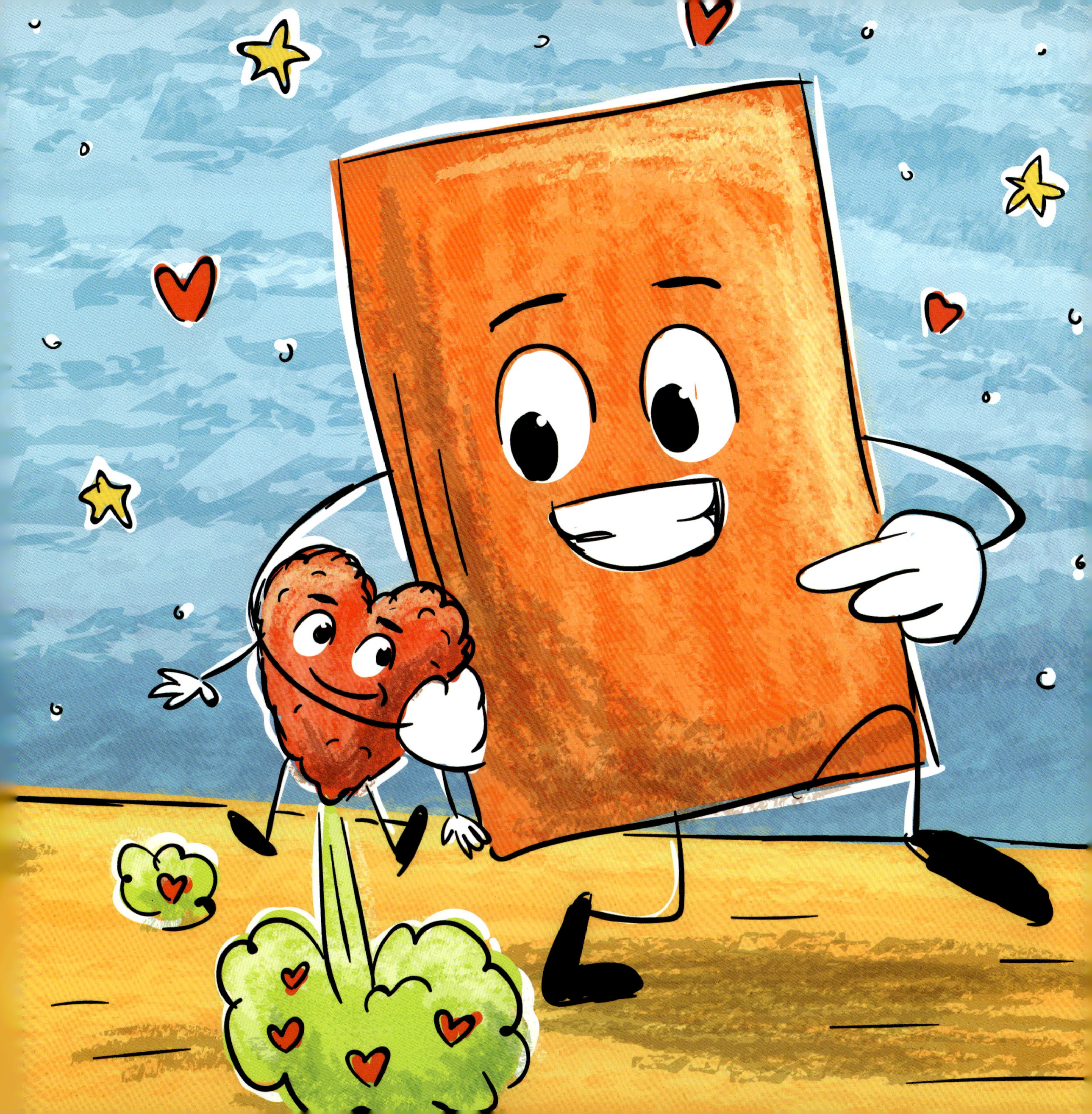

The heart can't help itself.
It has a lot of love to **share**.
When it's hugged so tightly,
It can't help but release some air.

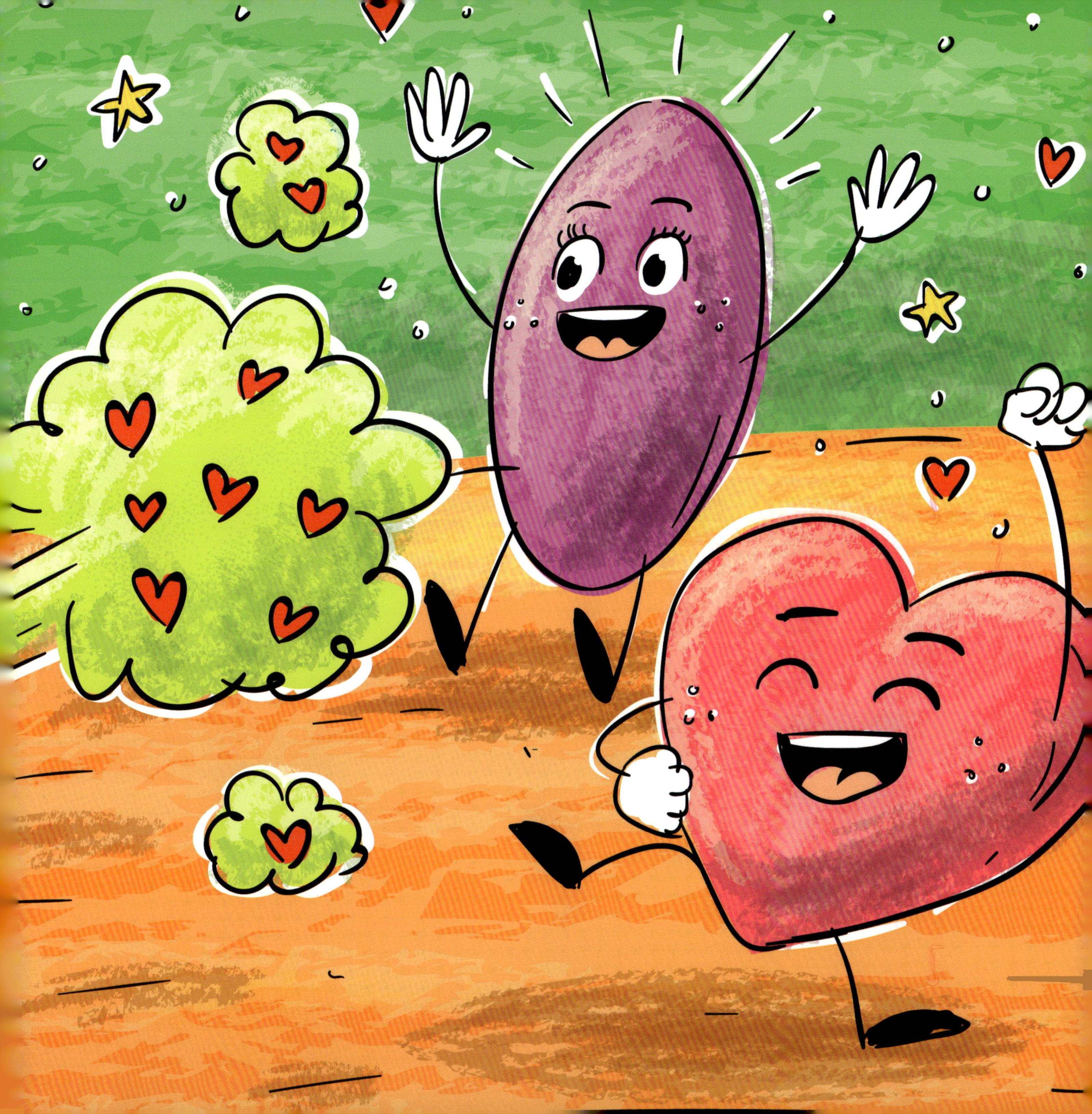

It's not always very loud,
Every now and then, you may hear a **POOF**!
The heart tries to hold it in,
But sometimes it accidentally goofs.

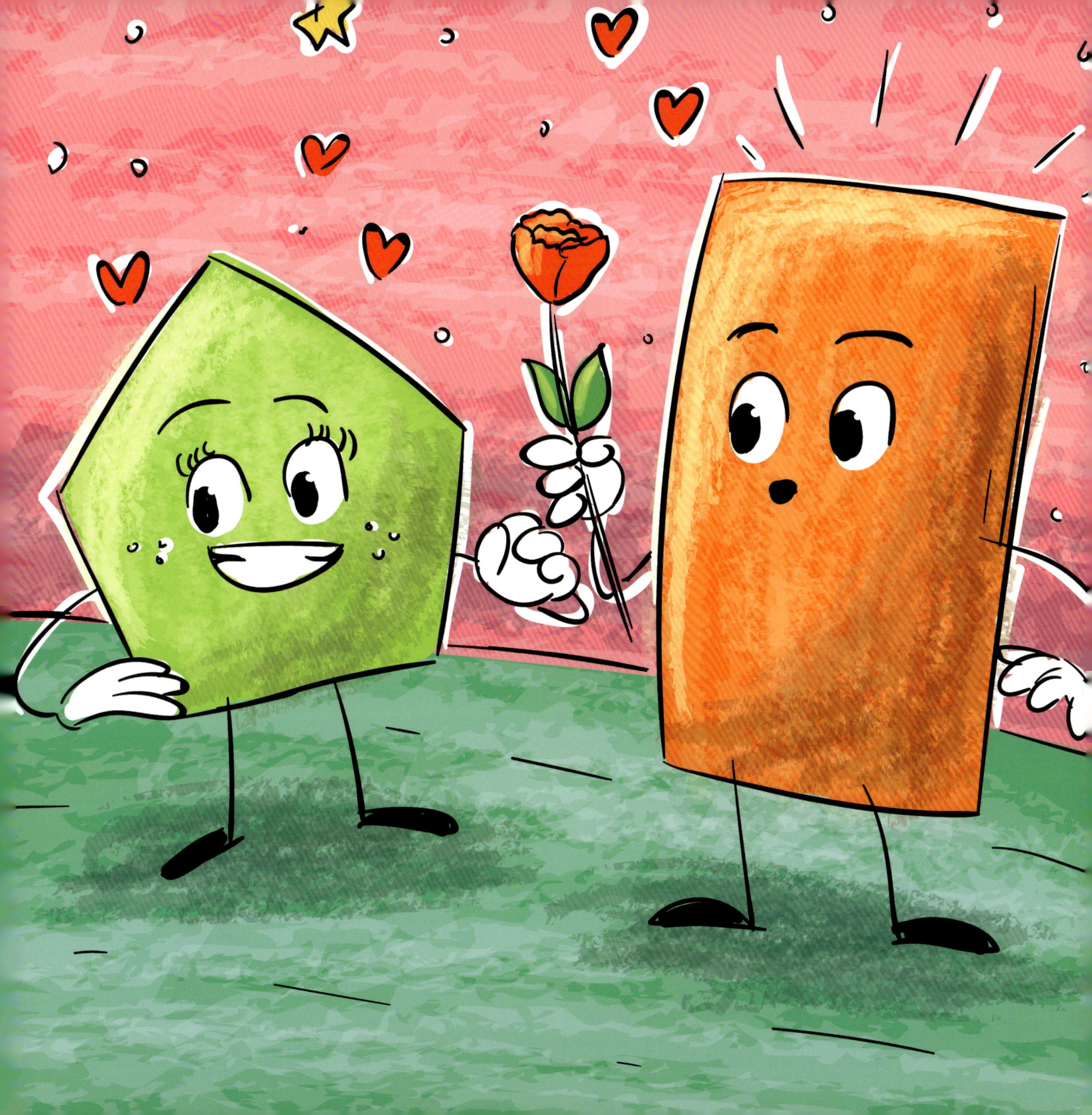

It only toots when it's **hugged**.
That seems to be the magic trick!
So when your farting heart toots
You don't need to be worried that it's sick.

That's actually how it expresses love.
It's a beautiful **reaction**.
Hopefully this natural burst
Does not bring you any dissatisfaction.

So if you want to know how much your heart loves you,
Just give it a really nice **squeeze**.
Listen for the love puff
And be happy with it, if you please.

Hug your Farting Heart,
Each and every day.
Especially hugging it harder
On **Valentine's Day**!